SCARECRONE

SCARECRONE

MELISSA BRODER

Publishing Genius Press
Baltimore

Published by Publishing Genius Press
Baltimore, Maryland
www.publishinggenius.com
First edition February 2014

Copyright © 2014 by Melissa Broder
All rights reserved
www.melissabroder.com

ISBN: 978-0-9887503-7-1

Cover design by Alex Merto
Page design by Adam Robinson

Distributed to the trade by Small Press Distribution
www.spdbooks.com

CONTENTS

ix	*Dark Poem*
1	Astral Locket
2	When I Hear the Word *Serenity* I Think *Doped*
4	Breathe Normally
5	The Great
6	How to Give Head to a Sick Person
7	Satisfy the Desolate
8	Light Control
9	Power Nothing
10	Tour
11	Sand Ceremony
12	Poem for My Son
14	Hi Humanity
15	Mud Rush
16	Dirt Nap
17	The Nature of Our Concerns
18	Living Downers
19	Today's Cauldron
20	Shiny Eyes
21	The Saint Francis Prayer Is a Tall Order
22	Judgment
24	Rave On
26	Donut
27	Proper Disposal of Holy Water
28	Exact Composition Is a Secret
30	Tender Black
32	A Preoccupation May Be Shared
34	Inflate the Slide
35	For the Real World
36	Consecration
37	Visible World
38	Power Animals
41	Penelope and Odysseus
42	Ask to Be Reseated
43	Knowledge Is Power No It's Not
44	Trompe L'oeil

45	Test for a Fault
46	Separable
47	Haul
48	Ventriloquism
49	This Activity Is Not Available
50	Letter From a Crone
51	Don't Make Me Grow
52	The Good Panic
54	Sutra
55	Mythic
56	Varieties of Religious Experience
57	The Other Exists as a Perfect Embodiment of Your Desire
58	Hip Older For Younger
59	Self-Portrait as Satan
60	Haunt
61	Transcendental Critique
62	Multicursal
63	Brother
64	Get Out of Your Whale Boat
65	Last Skin
66	Sky Mall
67	Sky Kids
68	Hope This Helps
69	Protrusion
70	Thousands
71	Powered
72	Blue and Green House
73	Ultimate Giver
74	From a Place Of ____?
75	Advaita
76	I Give a Convincing Sermon
77	The Purpose of Ritual
78	Prism Ditch
79	Daze Bones
80	Lost Choir
81	Cold Front
82	Spirit Fear
83	Forgotten Nothing

Tonight I've watched
the moon and then
the Pleiades
go down

The night is now
half gone; youth
goes; I am

in bed alone

— Sappho

DARK POEM

Today I sorted all-beef knockwurst
in bags of sauerkraut.
They were ancient knocks
too old for our humanity.
One small girl ate a fat knock
until she vomited light.
I watched her vomit in the dark
and felt I was owed a dark poem.
I kept saying *daughter daughter*
though I could never be a mother.
Light is every rainbow color.
I offered her my dark arm.
A poem kept us company.
It was dark as evidence.
Poetry is not evidence,
it is and it is not not not.
Somebody is lying
about the moon disappearing.
I offered her a cherry cola
to help her vomit darker.

SCARECRONE

ASTRAL LOCKET

She went into the silent room
and in the silent room there had never been a word
only the breath before the word

and she was deep within herself
her own breathing and the breathing of the world
the Earth swelling and pumping

thick blank in all canals
elevating her entire body
then vanishing her completely

and it felt good to be bodiless
in this pre-word vanishing

then she was offered up the men
one for each of the rest of her days
with their middle fingers and axes
hymnbones and ligaments

the men who meant an end to vanishing

for in the silent room
one must return all gifts
to make room for other gifts

a light for blood exchange

the chance to float in different ways
than the silence already floated her
which was already
so good

WHEN I HEAR THE WORD *SERENITY* I THINK *DOPED*

I am told to sit and wait for it
in the liturgy of moths
like there is even a choice
like if I called it would eclipse
my sad sack of dark words
no it would not
no it would not
every time I called it came
but not like a thunderhead
not the lasers I expected
always peoplewords
or some piece of person ripped sideways
sideways spirit
below as above
and no one is watching
but please believe it cares
I must believe it cares and cares
as hurt dots the sod
let my tongue unravel
to lick a milky cord
even as I waste my minutes
let me cream the cord
right to my heart
with syllable and spit
though it will never be what I want
and I am going to have to resemble me
as I came into this desert
broken up
and full of bones

like the universe is too big
to be seen all at once
like the whale was already written
like ok there is a light
but I cannot feel the nod
I will not get to feel the nod
and if I feel the nod
it isn't it

BREATHE NORMALLY

Give over your worries
but where? I have a condition
named plastic ceiling. My globe
is a snow one, my eyeballs
roll for what they desire
(OUT) but never alter
the border. Some watcher
gave me birth and water
and a replica of a church.
What the condition am I
supposed to do in here?
Life is a processional
in reaper's terms of getting
closer. Get closer slow
or fast. I go to the lip
of my own gap and peer
into the pore. I am wet
with no neighbor. Water
water. I'd learn to love
my neighbor if I had one.

THE GREAT

This is a conversation
I am conversing with The Great
Though I know no perfect talk exists
And if it does I will never talk perfect
I talk with snow in my mouth
I talk with snakes in my mouth
There are many greater mouths than mine
Can we still be friends?
Volition me to The Great!
I seek in garbage doors
This strange seeking is not without reason
For The Great has made a million dark and slimy charms
My palms are full of slimy cargo
I am carving my way to The Great
I am carving through my slimy body
When it breaks The Great floods in

HOW TO GIVE HEAD TO A SICK PERSON

I am going to grow you from a bean
and anything that I grow shall be mine
I will suck you from a bean
and I will suck you into a horn
and I will spell out i a m h e a l i n g y o u
I will do it with my tongue
this is not all I will do
but it is the last of my words
there have been so many words
falling over us like paper cutouts
there has been great disappointment
but here we are now
my elbows jut like strong wings
I am a very strong girl
look at what a woman you have
I am the priestess of resurrection
though I cannot make your body strong
I will make your heart loud
your heart is already so brave
you have given me so much power
you are my mother and my father
I am your dog and your daughter
look at how we are still alive
the clock is dead under the floor
and you go in the dark cavern of my mouth
and you go in the dark recesses of my mind
and you go and you go and you go and you go
and you go and you go and you go and you go

SATISFY THE DESOLATE

I call it sex
because I don't know
how else to say
terrified of dying.
Silence ruins
everything. It says:
you will not get your wings this way
not the wings you want
and you want
more than anybody.
I have wanted
many unfair things.
What is most unfair
is that the Earth is still okay
with me being here
I think, and even
encourages it.
Hello ocean
you have asked me
not to die, but I swim
in neon pools
that are happy
to kill me.

LIGHT CONTROL

I have never been inside myself

Another place wants me dead

It is built in a ring around my core

Like asking a donut how to live

It can only cry and be eaten

Don't you see

Angels have tried to help me

And I smiled for them

Feeling genuinely good and kind

Then after a while I got tired

Of being on good behavior

They never asked for perfection

But I felt I needed to perform

And the smile stayed no matter what I did

Even when dying improperly

I left everyone I knew in the other room

But I picked them back up again

Teach me to die teach me to die

I want to create a beautiful dying

The end will need to be dark and soft

Like walking home to your real mother

POWER NOTHING

When I say I am a fierce woman I mean I am a gentle woman.

When I say I am a gentle woman I mean leave me alone.

When I say leave me alone I mean I don't know what to do.

When I say I don't know what to do I mean HELP.

When I say HELP I mean I believe in something bigger.

When I say I believe in something bigger I mean because I want to.

When I say because I want to I mean because I need to.

When I say because I need to I mean to live.

TOUR

My heart has nine chambers.
One of them contains
a mirror. The other eight
I do not remember
ever being inside.

SAND CEREMONY

Do you believe in you

absolutely not

everything so beloved

but emptiness goes heyyy

I lead my army of nothing

the dogs of starlight nothing

I leave a lonely body

blank on the beach

the mouth flames out

I think *good*

one less hole to fall through

cracks in its babble

I was pouring out

another ghost with eyebrows

friends of friends of friends

the costume hair I wore

I was spilling out

every blackhole pore

I say *shut up shut up*

be real if you want

you can step into the sea

but the sea won't be there

POEM FOR MY SON

I am giving birth to a 22-pound baby
on the cusp of Pisces and Aries.
I will pretend he is Taurean.
We know with salvation
the sex of each child we carry.
We know what we want.
I exhale the word *Avram*
to breathe him into form.
I pour snow on his chart
to divine a life of civil service.
He will Mary Magdalene
all the brides on earth
in the space between their legs.
He will shoot them up
and walk them down a pink aisle.
Bridal headaches will fortell
reality beneath their veils.
They will stay brides for two years
then pay curfew to ooze.
My nurses twitch in purple scrubs
awaiting baby Avram.
They drink purple kool-aid
and eat powdered donuts.
They pour kool-aid in my mouth
to hurry out my breaths.
They pray over my gown
and I suckle on the donuts.

Cast out of my zodiac
for smelly food and coarse dreams
I was born a virgin.
I am proud to be
so delicate a mare today.
Take care of me I say
like it is nothing.

HI HUMANITY

I was
scared
my soul
would
never
call and
now it is
calling
and I
am like
shhhh

MUD RUSH

I have new commandments to help me love the wilderness
First commandment: never leave the wilderness
Make a fire or beget an image

I beget the fallen angel Azazel
We are kissing in a ditch
He cries for banging up his mother's heart

Every woman is the same woman
Azazel's mother is his wife
Who am I?

I can make tattoos out of berry juice and sticks
I tattoo crosses on Azazel's fingers
I make them so they look like anchors

Azazel sinks his anchor fingers in
I turn sapphire blue
His hands will not stay hooked

I stuff my holes with sticks
Then I burn down the wilderness
I burn mosquitos and flies

I burn wolfshit and trees
Azazel begins to choke in firelight
In this way he rises

DIRT NAP

Azazel's dead body rose
because Azazel was never
alive. I am alive
and this is also about me.
Highly sensitive persons
are angels. Let's give a shoutout
to softness. Humans please touch me
until I grow an adapter.
Fetch my dopamine blanket
the moon is in Aries
is in crisis. Azazel rose.
Azazel was colored bright orange.
The nozzle they twist on your lips
when you die makes your spirit
arcade off its hinges.
The body turns colors
that a spirit underneath
your spirit always wanted
to be. Azazel was
cantaloupe. Azazel was
tangerine. Break my spirit
I say break it now on a grave
or over the edge of
a casket. You will see it
was only a blemish.

THE NATURE OF OUR CONCERNS

This is a fire, a fire of learning
to die. Fuel the fire with no objects
specific to one generation
just a pyre of sitting
in the collected whispers
of all who have lived. Allow them
to frighten you with their having passed
and still keep sitting. Don't reach
for any clothes or tattoos,
you are always naked anyway
and yes you do
have angel wings
that grow heavy with love
sometimes. Love is all the time
if you are quiet. How much
are you quiet?

LIVING DOWNERS

Please don't call me out

I am getting worse

quiet fucks me good

but I can't hear

I make fake people in my serrated brain

and eat them with my one free mouth

their bones are tar

to fill me with no needle

the Buddha shakes his head

I hand him my holes

he drapes them over his shoulders

sits on the sky

the dust and sunlight

the pine trees and the fucking moon

if he can be still then good

if he can awaken then good

I am already growing more holes

and will not do the wait

in the temple of my jaw

I do not claim to be right

I am a lone wolf

I am a lonely wolf

I make people up

and I eat them

TODAY'S CAULDRON

Is this how shallow

my heart is yes

and no it is

all I have

so no

I say

I am glad

to live

but also

I think

I mean it

SHINY EYES

The difference between love and _____ is makebelieve.

Reality has meat but I don't care.

I sit with illusion for six days.

On the seventh day god calls me lost from within.

The god of love is maybe over me.

I hear the sky shut.

The god of love never gets over anyone.

I am the god of love.

You have to keep falling out.

I am so full of eyes I am going blind.

In the dark the god of love can find me.

Does it have to be silent?

I am going to go alltheway dark.

I think I am still holding on.

Even dead I am still here.

Even dead the light.

THE SAINT FRANCIS PRAYER
IS A TALL ORDER

Mostly it's hard to believe
what matters is in your heart.
I'll remember for an hour.
I'd like to tell god what god's will is.
I'd like for god to make god's tongue
really fast and gentle on my—
sorry if this isn't scripture.
I tried / I'm tired
and I ate up all the begats.
To be a saint is to be courageous
about the pursuit of what?
I have a pretty mouth.
Meet me at the black clock.

JUDGMENT

When the shaman comes to town I try to hump the shaman
I try to hump angels
I cannot untouch sublime beings

My guardian angels are mine and all for me
When they leak they leak me
Still there are cracks between us
And you have to fill up cracks with candy

If I am not allowed candy I use my body
If I am not allowed my body I use the internet
Television is going to deliver me from the internet
The angels pray over my screens

My angels are probably lonely
Also disillusioned with me
I have always felt the presence of a disappointed being

The shaman says I am not dead
I am definitely dying
I am already digging out of my coffin

I dress in cicada skins
I go bright blonde
Above me is the blonde angel Raphael
And I try to make the blonde angel french me

The blonde angel has a thick tongue
He wants to talk about healing
The violence no one has done to me

Every violence I have done to me
When I leak I leak me
What was so hell that I violenced me
That I knifed the wounds into my wings

There were always beautiful horses
There were cracks in all the horses
When I stuffed their mouths with candy
They turned to rotten

I made candy luncheons in the pasture
It tasted very desire
I poured cherry soda into all my cracks

Tell the angels to give me sugar
If they do not want to hump me
A supreme being should heal me
But only for forever

RAVE ON

Kids they are kids
they are 18 17 16 15
and the globe bloats
with their sunglasses.
I am after hours.
I am 97 98 99 100.
I am looking
through the clouds
on the flipside
of their teething.
Never am I
less dayglo.
I will gag
the universe
till it tongues me
back into babyface.
Who knows where
the universe lives
the way up
to its mouthhole?
Some old god
should young me up
an ancient Satan
with a deathbone.
He will probe
my throat
and whisper

I am glad you feel
good in spots
and awful
in other spots.
He will say
what did you
expect?

DONUT

Thirsty for milk and humping
god's knee till god feels like a doll
passed from suffering person
to suffering person.
I have never loved in a way
that wasn't gorged or object-y
but I'm getting better
at praying for all humankind
in the dawn before I eat
the sun. No god wants to be
an old man with balls down
to his knees and I don't either
I don't think. I waver because
you shouldn't just fill one space
with the unclarity of another.

PROPER DISPOSAL OF HOLY WATER

When I purge the abscess of a girlhood
I am heavier a female.
Thick lips belch the zeros
of my previous condition.
The headmistress of space and time
lavishes gravity like a bear.
You can be blessed at every altar
and a grunt in waking life
but I am one woman now
from scalp to toenails
teeth to pussy.
This new opacity makes the misplaced years
my entire education seem an imp
a hollow tool
really gone.
On to piss the fountains
bust through my smocks
in gleeful fat and torpor.
The harp of the flesh is no illusion
or phenomenon reserved for babies.
Rain in every hole
butter on each finger
in every breast a spit of felines
once you stop the search.
Don't go
to the swamps for medicine
or to the streams with eyes on elixir
but into the balm of your own robe.
After the family hatchet
the black air of schoolmates
who said serenity in withered books
miles of that river drain.

EXACT COMPOSITION IS A SECRET

Invent a fantasy to save me
and project it on another body.

I don't think I am worthy of rescue.

Humble me down so low
that this small bread
feels like an orgasm.

That is how we enjoy the world.

I see lovers
and they are not real.
I mean they are real
but my eyes are not.

Once upon a time the world rose
to meet my plasticine eyes.

The oceans flooded
and carried me away
and I said *thank you lord*
for making this possible.

Then I washed up on the shore
and had to start walking
through an island jungle again:
barefoot, pale and salty.

I cried
but not because I was lost.

I cried
because my body
was not waterlogged enough
to fall right off the bone.

TENDER BLACK

Nobody bleeds white like I bleed white

Into a ditch the shadow of my bloodbag is white

I want a darker aura, like I want it to be gorgeous

Pour out light but pour shiny black

Nobody believes you when you say you are bad

I do not believe I am fully recovered

I can't get my footing so I grab for a human

All the wrong animals and I am wrong

I am wrong in a bomb and also on the crucifix

I am wrong in the penalty for light, which is knives

You must get a weapon or nobody sees you

Germs are promising they are my only sperm

Spit in a ditch and grow a new you

I promised myself there would be no fucking

Rats are doing it over and over

So you see it is not my fault

Let the brain do what it wants it will

Blankety blank blank and plenty of pigs

Cactuses I ate and then spit up

Carcasses of everyone we've ever been

My carcasses are rags baby plug me into castle

Fingers are for lots of things but I only see one use

Everything has cracks in it okay okay

I've never been a circle but I want to fill it now

A PREOCCUPATION MAY BE SHARED

I saw time fold into a carful of women and they dropped their lips like husks.

I'm afraid of turning purple.

I don't want to hear any alarms under my hair.

O sanctus sanctus sanctus varicosis-minimus lolitas roseus coralus salmonus tightest pinkest jonbenet jonbenet jonbenet.

PINK — 1. Pale red. 2. The highest degree. 3. Prime. 4. To prune or trim. 5. Beefcheeks' maiden voyage.

There is no need to be pink when another woman is already pink.

Jealous women jealous me into being jealouser.

If I soften I get to meet Joan of Arc.

We snow into an ashtray till she asks whose ashtray is this?

You must learn to love all the women.

I am proud of my me in Joan's hair tonight.

I am proud of my no-game.

The universe hums a dirge to clocks but so what?

Well ok I care.

I will maybe stop being of service to illusion.

I am interested in the ways that numbers fail.

Heaves of mourners form villages around the dead numerals.

At the funeral I finally find my eyes.

The game of my small coal needs drops down.

I am defrocked by prayer emergency.

The nudity is a wholesome pyre.

INFLATE THE SLIDE

Trade a man
who loves you
for language
I am addicted
to my thoughts
when our world
blows up
there is a pink bed
and two girls
sitting crosslegged
in pink smoke
meditating
on my dick
they feed him
strawberry yogurt
he gives them
chimeras

FOR THE REAL WORLD

I am waiting for somebody imaginary
to come back to me.

A woman
with supper breasts
depresses.

A man
who keeps shaving
burns me
out.

My imaginary person
never cooks an egg
but everyone else
does.

Everybody cooks an egg
even if they
don't.

I want to love in a place
that is contingent
on nothing.

I want to forge a union of nothing.

People don't want
to become
imaginary.

People are planning
trips to real places
and it's awful.

CONSECRATION

Yes I put myself here
I was having a terror time
I made a muscle
out of every trashy wing
and crawled to you
and your soft dick is shit to me
holy shit
in this way
I am sucking on your shit
I am trying to help your softshitdick
reach a miracle dimension
and I don't blame you
for being unwilling
to comply with my dream
the world is real
you are there
you like living
in the end
I don't want to make the grass
I don't want to go under it
zen is not for me
you are not for me
I hear dogs inside of me
some are good and some are wrong
I keep feeding the wrong dogs

VISIBLE WORLD

I bang
my forehead
on a thing
then go oops
the sky
it looks like
sheet rock
or a joke
it is
the sky
I am
waiting
on a stroke
maybe
chandeliers
up there
magick
is for people
who do not
believe
it all
is already
here
when
they build
a lab
that burps
goodwill
I will
worship
science

POWER ANIMALS

What kind of words do hawks use

My husband has a busted lifeline

A hawk beats its wings over his palm

Squawks *make it grow make it grow*

*

These are words hawks use without fear

My husband is deaf to feathers

I wave at him with my arms

*

We go to a glass mansion

We are not wealthy enough to enter the glass door

A hawk flies us through a window

And the hosts are delighted to have a poet in their circle

They make me give a recital by the glass fire

Then they shoot my husband with a glass rifle

Calling me derivative

As he bleeds all over their glass sofa

*

Wealthy women ask me where my baby is

I point to my dead husband

They ask *where is the jaguar on your jaguar*

I say *I have an alligator*

The wealthy women want to go to Rome to eat

I only eat frozen things

I ride my alligator the wrong way down a one-way street

*

My husband lies in the street

He begs me to bury him

I say *no*

*

A hawk issues the call:

Do not mess with this one

She will turn you into bad art

*

(BAD ART HORSEWISH INCANTATION)

horse farm horse farm

cottage with ponies

stallion bungalow

thoroughbred yurt

will work for mares

no skills

muck girl

dead meat

die in sleep

cowboy fantasy

magick forest

crystalline dream

unicorn

getting better

spirit horse

h e l p m e

*

Horses are made of words

You can assemble a mare or a stallion

You can make the bedroom have an ocean

I ride an Arabian down the bedpost

I nod at my dead husband

He rots on the carpet

I say *make it grow make it grow*

He says *no*

PENELOPE AND ODYSSEUS

Penelope is waiting and she is wet.
What else do we know about Penelope?
Is she braising a lamb shank to lure Odysseus?
O yeah, a lamb shank, it makes Odysseus wet.
His stomach grows heavy but he still can make rain.
He rains down on Penelope and dissolves her.
Odysseus and Penelope dissolve together.
Their stomachs are very heavy but they fly.
They fly around the whole world over every ocean.
When they fly over the deserts Odysseus laughs.
He feels he is the wettest juiciest lamb shank.
He believes he will never be dry again.
Odysseus will have to make rain again.
Odysseus will have to make rain again and again.
Odysseus's face becomes a black desert.
He asks Penelope to leave the sky.

ASK TO BE RESEATED

Dirt coat blankets the universe
and I pillow asteroid
with pervasive sense
an explosion is missing
rejection-sensitivity
soothed by palm trees
Pantheism
nice trip to CVS
vanity reasserts itself
when pain subsides
I could build a theater
around your head
perform the violence island
I was never taught to latch
I was born
latching

KNOWLEDGE IS POWER NO IT'S NOT

Obsession is my weather forecast.

The object keeps raining.

Shut me up with a computer.

Give me more than my share of you.

Revolution is coming for my pillow.

Can you make the revolution come fast?

Throw me in an unmarked van with my leather shoes.

Talk to me about free thought.

I am frightened of revolution.

I am frightened to be seen through the eyes of a dog.

So boring boring and full of black instruments.

The instruments pixelated like yours.

We are fucking in an unmarked van.

Only one flame of eros gets lit.

You try to choke me and buy me a seltzer.

I choke on the possible air.

Porn is the weatherman.

You change coats again again.

Talk to me about free love.

The revolution will change me for five minutes.

TROMPE L'OEIL

I really love your work
the way it is nailed by its wrists
to a cross
I mean to say
the way it gushes
from nothingness
but words make a meal of me
chomp chomp
and isn't it Jesus
everybody is buzzing about
the way he did not use
a microphone
and did not own a camera
to self-record the curtaining
of himself
as he knew himself
tremoring up there on the grain
how did he wait for it
I cannot imagine
I can only make a small map
of my fingerprints
which are your fingerprints
and a roof
which is a human roof
and tell you
how good it is
to have a roof
before the sky

TEST FOR A FAULT

Every airplane is sleep.

I point my finger at a jetliner to rest my eye.

Boys smell holes in a neon blue banner I keep in my wallet.

The banner says RELAX GOD IS IN CHARGE.

Stephen Dedalus you are never on my mind.

You come to my island and I am the island.

You are well-traveled but that is arid.

My eye is on the sky.

I say *Helios.*

You say *Apollo.*

I say *Charybdis.*

You say *I'll show you hetero.*

This instant must be sustained.

I pour black flower milk into a goblet but you refuse to hallucinate.

The breeze sounds an alarm.

I tongue your overlip in an air raid.

You go to the sea to swim with Calypso.

Crocodiles rattle shells.

I look at you long through my one eye.

You become the island.

SEPARABLE

What we have here is an opportunity
to make contact with language, which professes
to love us. I am actually still deciding
if I am going to stick with language, its tongue
and teeth are so peopled and I feel
the universe is trying to ask me
something else through rings on the ceiling, heat,
nameless fruit that drops through the window.
Yes I live in a body and am now being asked
to assess what my experience was like before.
It made me feel okay, oh I was so okay
that when I first got bodied I died.

HAUL

Hello porn video.
Hello scarecrone
on the train.
You know we got old.
The young are devils
in our dream.
They are made of rotten sugar.
We are holding onto one car
and the car is named *tight*
like a baby. Call me
tight like a baby.
Clarity is a wart.
You see the warts
on my face? Eat them
retrospectively. Save me
scarecrone. The condition
of my face. I ate
the world and I ate
the world. It tasted
like a bandage.

VENTRILOQUISM

The gap between motherhood
and no motherhood
is grip. I wield my eggs
against women who have
dried up. Mine will dry
on a river rock, punish
my future body
for taking the river
for granted. Hold my
palms up to the Goddess
and say *Tell me what to do*.
If the Goddess wants me
knocked up I'll be a fish. If
she wants me in the river
I'll be wetter. She calls me
daughter. A man becomes
an infant in my lap.

THIS ACTIVITY IS NOT AVAILABLE

A fire ritual
burns hot little graves
for my electrons.
Sear those electrons
I don't care my womb
is wordless anyway.
Once I picked out names
girth necks the color
of their irises.
Last of the line last
of the line I'll wear
my dust like petals.

LETTER FROM A CRONE

When you get old the autumns come
bearing black pistachios

which are not more delicious than green ones
but they are very good.

Do not forget you can find your way home
by saying *thank you I love you help me*.

Put the note in god's bra

and poof you are in your nucleus
with big dreams again.

You were despondent
when you were no longer young

but now you are hooked up to a river.

DON'T MAKE ME GROW

A mustardseed of okayness. We're here
to know our own goodness. I have barely
cried at all. I spent so much time away
from me that when I finally feel me
I might kill me. I guess you sit
with you and see you do not kill you.
Then you live. No nothing
will give me that okayness.
I want bodies packed
around my body. A layer
is missing. The air is so
dangerous. Blink twice
you're off the path.

THE GOOD PANIC

Vortexes are pouring out
of my stomach into
my throat because: unknown.
*Don't worry, under the dying
is sadness,* says love. No
that is me talking. *Sometimes
you just get sick, even
in the mind, and there is nothing
you can do.* That is love
talking. Love, relieve me
of my fear of fear and of
my fear of everything. Do it
on your time as I know
you will. May I find you
on the internet in words
from a stranger. This is how
you work like a lattice, not
from the top down. Lay me up
so I may know my power-
lessness and therein find
my iron. Needles in my hands,
needles in my feet. Little body
pitched into the pines of having
ever been born. Big body
smeared around little body
and full of stars and horses
and fingers of everyone
who has ever touched me.
Love, you keep touching me.
Hallways of my brain filled

with wormtracks like a condom
over the light. Shitbags
in the trees. Water water
now love water water.
My mouth is wide.

SUTRA

Be alive briefly. Let the light love you
till you can something something.

Chant to make meaning
but you are no creator
only the want of more time
only no sun and an egg
and nothing is coming
to rescue you from the cosmos.

The cosmos is vomiting all over
your legs, upchucking black blood
and cosmic upchucks suck they don't even make
fun sounds, just coughs so fuck that cosmos
and its lame gushes. Fuck its vagina.

The cosmos made you without your consent
coughed you out then stuck you in a bow
and what a gift, a gift to be regifted,
a gift that will annul itself for stars.

MYTHIC

The universe is vacant
because I am
here.

I brought my holes and all the men
flew up inside.

What got left behind are women
who will save me.

I want to lick a cosmic titty
because god built me
with these holes

so I am coming for you god

if you are the mad cow
then I am your wayward calf

if you are the mother
I say MORE LOVE NOW

and if you are the father
then bounce me on your knee
till I feel it in my holes
because that is where
I need to
feel it.

VARIETIES OF RELIGIOUS EXPERIENCE

I don't know. Humans
are always waiting for
something to stuff our
holes. Even when I have
a man in my holes I
am leaking and begging
for other. Moonlight
mushrooms. Once upon
a time I ate them and
saw the way I looked
as a baby. Light bulbs
had blue veins inside
that is how alive
everything was.
Still I wanted a man
to give me my name.
God was showing me
the code through a prism.
I fractured the glass
on purpose because
I did not want to know.

THE OTHER EXISTS AS A PERFECT EMBODIMENT OF YOUR DESIRE

A separation of the speaker
from herself across time
so I am me who is no one
in black velvet hunched over
carnations. I want a hot shaman
to sew my lips together and say
HEAL. When a man is just a head
it's intimate. I'd love to watch
your head suck a big tank
of holy water. Instead my eye
is crying into a plastic cup.
It doesn't matter if I search
or stop. The house is going
to levitate or it is not.
No medicine man ever
told me his secret. I drew
a heart myself and licked it.

HIP OLDER FOR YOUNGER

Dark piano enters as ode
to maggots. Maggots
rise with streamers
to my skull. Boyfever
eviscerates maggots
through magick
breath of pizza
no ash. I rain ash
on boy sunglasses
to deceive his eyes.
Why don't you give me
a kiss? Why don't you
give me a tomb? Look
it's a funeral procession.
Don't bring a baby here.

SELF-PORTRAIT AS SATAN

My wings are made of garbage

At least they can be touched

I want you I want you

Especially the old and ugly

Take these bottles of soda

And tubes of cherry lipstick

These are my demon breakfast

And my red red hooves

It is better to be satan

With half-trash filling

Than try to stuff your holes with clouds

Lacerating on your nails

I once stuffed my holes with halos

Until honey dripped down

The honey smelled like village women

Full of want and feces

Village women screaming out for anything alive

I shut them up with jars of eye cream

And a plastic head

I gave them eggs of pantyhose

And a melting cathedral

I gave them black snakeskins

And menstrual sponges

I gave them sainted men

With semisoft dicks

Making it hard

To feel totally fucked

HAUNT

When I was born
a man died wheezing
to make room for me
on the green islands
over the ocean.
I see him in the mirror
and repeat
I did not choose
still a choke
grows inside me
so brittle it is a bush.
I don't want to see any more
of god's green factory.
Trees are a trigger
as are vines.
Anything with petals
must be zapped
look how the grass
grows in knives.
Vitality comes
with too much skull
and an evil rose on its lips.
Lace may be safe.
Daisies
are off limits.

TRANSCENDENTAL CRITIQUE

As always there is schism
between skeleton
and never asking for a skeleton
tearing around the kitchen.
You enter with biscuits
and each contains a gemstone
that tastes like its color:
ruby is cherry,
pink tourmaline pussy.
The word for wish is want.
Knowledge gets us what?
Not enough biscuits.
Sick dogs sniff each other out.
I build an oven over your mouth
and set the door on fire.
Grunts are still possible.
Let's corpse.

MULTICURSAL

I am walking alone
through a dark forest.
I have to stop for each rock
in my chest or else
they grow bigger than me.
Caked in ribs the rocks
of desire are hot
for all the wrong
trees. These rocks have burned
a long time. I stop
for 21 seconds
each time. I am only
allowed 21 seconds
or the trees will kill me.

BROTHER

How is your crown supposed to fall off
when you look like Jesus
I am superficial because it feels religious
let's light a candle for you not wanting me back
we could be dirty juice and bent crucifix
suspend the alphabet now
o sanctus sanctus sanctus puer
mea illusio mea est mea omnia
can you believe in guides your eyes can't see
can you believe I still want you
I cannot believe you would choose loneliness
loneliness is how little you want me
I know little of Christianity
so I love it
take me behind your mouth
that I might forsake it
pillar of salt
pillar of salt

GET OUT OF YOUR WHALE BOAT

Now is no time for pity and compunction.

I will carry you around like a baby.

You are a piggie and I will eat you.

Savages are infinitely happier.

I would abandon my island for you.

(This is probably untrue.)

I have such mosquito innards.

My bone condition is suck.

Let me other you out of your skeleton.

You are calico cotton and powder.

Let me throw my fire body on you.

You will never tell others *don't be afraid*.

There are so many ways to row away.

I can't even make new language for it.

I am tired of want so I use old language.

Old language is old and mine to use.

LAST SKIN

I am in the hotel of bodies
temporarily. Love is
millions of needles but really
none. Dark crow, cackle cackle,
the pyramids already fell.
Leave my eye and join the light.
Don't you know I craned my neck
for saints outside. Don't you know
I felt like crying. There were bats
in my ribcage and I didn't even know.
Behind them my soul was snowing.

SKY MALL

There once was a sky full of boys.
Gravity is a vile invention
when time owns the ground.
Every field is raked with clocks.
Turnips wave a white flag.
Potatoes are bombs.
I explode them in my mirror
to fly the glass.
I fly to the leopard coast.
The scarecrone is old and dull.
Dig, she says.

SKY KIDS

You didn't know
I was unreal

I am the worst
body

nobody ever
taught me dopamine

I want to drink
your star jelly

HOPE THIS HELPS

We need a loving grownup to give us advice
and that loving grownup is the universe.
Who wants to go to the universe for help?
You can't touch the universe
or kiss its mouth
or stick your fingers in its mouth
though sometimes the universe works
horizontally through people
and I like that.
A human channeled the universe
when he said I was milk.
The human said I was born milk
but then grownups poured in lemon juice
which makes sense
because I've always felt like rotten cottage cheese
and I've been running around the planet
like I don't want to be this
when in fact I am milk
and was always milk
and will always be milk.
I don't think this is a story blaming grownups
for the ways we are ruined.
I think this is a story about knowing
what we are up against
mostly ourselves
and what our essential consistency is
which in my case is milk
and in your case is milk
you are milk you are
milk you are
so milk.

PROTRUSION

I hold my legs

like two chicken drumsticks.

I could rip them off.

I am capable

of nothing

but black words

on a white tongue.

God gave me a red tongue

and only god knows

who god is.

Bring me a priest

gushing off

in the moonlight

with fishies that go

for a night swim

so I with open mouth

praying over

a dead rose

can gulp

that ocean butter up

and swell

like a baleen whale.

THOUSANDS

He is told to send a lock of hair
but instead sends a dossier
of charts. There are bullets,
vectors, single choice answers.
No questions. On every page
appears a yellowish husband.
The husband is a sick man.
I want the diagram-sender
sicker. I want every man
fainting in a reservoir
of contaminated water.
I have black chrysanthemums
in each hole and a gypsy smell.
My climax shakes the basin.
I hold out one hand for every man
but I'm looking at my snake.

POWERED

A lamp powered by blood is called

a miracle and a legend

powered by blood is called a church.

I am not against anything

not even infinity. I

just don't want to be made to watch.

My consort's head is burning hot

so I take it off. This is not

how compassion works but it works.

What of next? Next the headless man

and I go dancing on a death

till we're dumb dumb dumb and blonde blonde.

Oh how I love a dumb blonde neck.

No universe tells it to stop

and put an apple in its mouth.

BLUE AND GREEN HOUSE

I am in a house
I can see the sofa from here
There are no pictures
He owns all the windows
There is no mother in the house
All the clocks are dead
Curtains are a reflex
Dinner is cardboard
I want to lay quiet
In a bowl of batter
I want to shine His hands
With my hair
He begins to cut
He saws and grunts
And takes off limbs
My mouth is gone
I am too loud for a mouth
I am too wet for a crown
Every wire hangs
I spark and spark all over
The dog is burping dogshit
He loves and loves his master
I am afraid
Jesus is a man

ULTIMATE GIVER

I ask my father not to set fire to the house and it snows on us.

It snows ashes of all the cigarettes he has ever smoked.

My father was a renaissance man and his cigarettes were lords.

Mouths were ladies.

I lay out blankets so my father will be more comfortable in the snow.

I lay the blankets beside a china set.

My dead husband and I got it for our wedding.

My dead husband climbs in bed with my father, shattering the cups.

Their sweat drips through the blankets.

In the morning I write the men a letter that reads:

Dear darlings, time is ugly no?

I am a romance addict, which is neither of your faults but the fault of time.

I am an everything addict, which may be one of your faults.

Mostly it is the fault of god who made me.

Do you want to have dinner?

We can eat in a hallway or in the cigarette bed.

I have no fruits but I have a horse.

We can use his meat.

This is not the kind of love Jesus was talking about.

I am full of teeth.

FROM A PLACE OF _____?

I opened my eyes on day 0
and said to the universe SHAKE ME
and the universe complied
which felt too real
so I built another universe
within the universe
and crawled inside

and I keep thinking
my little universe
is the only universe
but then I think no
this is not the universe at all
it is destruction

when in truth
everything is the universe
my little universe
and the big universe

and when I ask the big universe
what it wants from me
it says so easily
become a channel

but mostly I think
the universe just wants me here
so I am here
in a pain
of my making

ADVAITA

I will never return to this body
I wish I could love it more
the gurgle and the groan
the good groan and the bad groan
and also non-duality
but I love eternity in you
and on you
the plastic teeth you have constructed
to defeat a shitting clock
you bite it with fake fangs
and drink hot crystal time
and offer incantations
to give the vast some syntax
but only babble comes
and you have no need to sleep
and you miss the deepest pain
that comes from dreams
you shriek
to wash your garments
once again in bleach
begin another cycle

I GIVE A CONVINCING SERMON

I give a convincing sermon. I say *The body*
is a coat. It is a very dark and heavy coat
but worthless. Mother Mary nods from the pews.
If I give Mary all my atoms she will plant them
in a garden where ripened women relinquish
their bones to make room for littler women.
It is dangerous to grow accustomed to a garden.
Just when the flowers soften you, they disappear.
Then you are a weepy fern among skyscrapers.
I don't want my soul exposed like that.
Neither can you make a garden stay. Don't even try.
Every plot becomes a dark city over time.
I have collected many dark ideas over time.
I have so many ideas they are a second coat.

THE PURPOSE OF RITUAL

When you fled I disappeared
into the abcesses of my brain.
We are both impulsive humans
and perhaps my disappearance
was premature. To reappear
I had to grow younger. I began
consuming images of boys
at a very rapid speed, never
their bodies just reflections.
I distorted all the mirrors
in mucus, oil and blood.
When I say that I consumed
I do not mean that I ate the mirrors,
only that I stood beside the boys,
dowsed the glass and incanted.
I chanted *you love me you love me*
to 3000 boys but none said yes.
What does it mean to be so sick
with want that you create rituals
which lead nowhere? Only to be
human, I think, and less ok
than animals. I don't want
to be human anymore
so I have covered the mirrors
in blankets. You returned to me
but never uncovered them.

PRISM DITCH

What I am saying is doomed:
men in tunnels running headfirst into trains
with grins on their faces.

Men lay out the wine and incense
for my memorial service.
I wanted there to be no wine
but I am dead.

I sleep on my hair like a wolf.
I knock against the shells
of cicada-men.

Have you ever crawled inside a shell?
It is the end of an image
you projected and adored.

The image was ripe
and full of protein
but people kept mouthing
the word *surrender*
which you must have heard
because you killed it.

I killed a pinkish man.
I popped the bubble of his head
with a safety pin.

This released a ticker
bleating *you you you you*
and all the ink
that poured from his mouth
I had written.

DAZE BONES

Notgod set me on fire and was like good luck

I think the shirt you wear is ultimate

When it turns red nothing can walk soft

Maybe birth me up on your fingers

You taste like not-sober alcoholics

Various breeds of errors and the way I feel you

No human power no human power

I cannot go there with you and I cried

The other life I was so nauseous

You didn't know I almost threw up

What if I threw up on your tongue?

When I put you in my mouth I got better

Forgive every body its mouth

I talk like I am sister heaven

I am really sister darkness

I am both at once and you are also

You didn't know you were an echo

In the dust I'll kill you up

I think you learn by unbeing

Like first you die and then go oh

LOST CHOIR

Every funeral is fake

Be a fake eulogy for me

Dig up the fake black flowers

Nothing left for me to almost say to you

Warm for me now

Say how good I really was

How I became my own Eskimo

The misguided knives

The sweet trash fires

Igloo of trauma and smiles

Igloo of poison and hair

So many shirts and mortal fucking love

I know it's funny cos turns to dust

The garbage kingdom everywhere

All the while the light

COLD FRONT

This is the light god has given you
so take it. What if
it is not enough?
There is never enough anything.
I am calling from the mountain.
I have reached the summit
and it's empty. I arrived
with war paint on my face.
I arrived starving.
My bag is filled with plastic dolls
I cannot eat. Garbagebody
latching onto things of things.
Plastic arms and real arms,
perfume veins. The vanished trail
for one that is always. The dust
coming and coming.

SPIRIT FEAR

The room where I will die is everywhere
I am hiding from a signal on the road
Signal from the angels or signal from the mother
Signal from the dog who is a wolf who is me
Signal from myself that I gag not to hear
Signal from the Earth and under the Earth
And I hear the roar of the walls
I eat a young man in the room of my death
I make everyone into a lantern
I make pockets of darkness so the room looks like heaven
And I declare my love to the darkness
Its cocks and its holes like my cocks and my holes
Stick a rag in my mouth for my lover
Make the dead smell like the dead

FORGOTTEN NOTHING

Can you die with the Earth
yes I can die
green green grass make me make me

I am going to become something pure and true
I am built for becoming
though I was made came
I unknew my arrival because
I unknew the way

I say nobody knows the way besides the way
I say once was lost but now am lost

I say never asked to wake
please make the waking gentle
for this woke child with shut eyes

Melissa Broder is also the author of *Meat Heart* (Publishing Genius, 2012) and *When You Say One Thing But Mean Your Mother* (Ampersand Books, 2010). She lives in the United States.

ACKNOWLEDGMENTS

Thank you to the following journals, in which some of these poems first appeared:

Better; BOMB; Books & Culture; Coconut; Columbia: A Journal of Literature and Art; Death Hums; Fence; Gigantic; Ghost Proposal; The Good Men Project; Green Mountains Review; Housefire; Illuminati Girl Gang; The Iowa Review; Jai Alai; Lungfull; NAP; Paperbag; Poets.org; Sixth Finch; Washington Square; Yalobusha Review

Love and thanks to Nicholas Poluhoff, Adam Robinson, Elaine Equi, David Groff, Alex Merto, Kristen Iskandrian, Lorian Long, Shoshanna Must, Margaret Curry, Steve Rosenthal, Danniel Schoonebeek, Sasha Fletcher, Arthur Seefahrt, Tyler Crawford, Gene Morgan, Mrs. Hovey, Linda and Robert Broder, Hayley Broder.

RECENTLY FROM PGP

You Can Make Anything Sad, poems by Spencer Madsen

Figures for an Apocalypse by Edward Mullany, a book of poems and short fictions

Activities, a comic book by John Dermot Woods

Fun Camp, a novel by Gabe Durham

I Don't Know I Said by Matthew Savoca, a novel

A Mountain City of Toad Splendor, a book of poetry and short fictions by Megan McShea

Night Moves, a conceptual ode by Stephanie Barber

Proving Nothing to Anyone by Matt Cook, a book of poems in five sections

Meat Heart, poetry by Melissa Broder

Old Gus Eats, a chapbook by Polly Duff Bresnick

Pee On Water, short stories by Rachel B. Glaser

please visit www.publishinggenius.com